W9-AHU-489

Paddle America

A Guide to Trips and Outfitters in all 50 States

Nick Shears

Starfish Press
Washington, D.C.

Paddle America
A Guide to Trips and Outfitters in all 50 States

Published by:
Starfish Press
6525 32nd St., N.W.
P.O Box 42467
Washington, D.C. 20015

Copyright © 1992 by Nicholas Shears
Library of Congress Card Catalog Number: 91-75664
ISBN 0-9622806-5-8
Printed in the United States of America

Front cover: A paddle crew on a Whitewater Voyages' trip drifts through a calm stretch between rapids on the renowned Class V Forks of the Kern, Sequoia National Forest, California. Photo by Barry Tessman.